Romantic Italian

Words & Sayings

True Italian Quotes with English translation. Learn the most romantic, sweet and passionate sayings we use in Italy.

+1000 phrases about love, family and life

You can find the audio and more contents on:

www.neeoart.com/italy

Contents

" L'arte degli italiani sta nella bellezza "
" The art of the Italians is in beauty "

- Kahlil Gibran

Introduction

Ciao! Hello! I'm Isabella, I'm an Italian girl born and raised in Italy. I wrote this book because I am in love with my country and with my language and I want to communicate to you, as an Italian, the wonders of Italy. Many times I read English translations of Italian texts or phrases and I realise how little they reflect the original meaning. Italian is a very complex language and if you are not a native speaker it's difficult to translate all its nuances of meaning. I hope that by reading this book you'll be able to appreciate a little more the deep and passionate meaning that expressions of love have in Italian.

Italy is a wonderful place, there is nothing in the world like it, it enters your heart and you will never forget it.

In the years that I lived abroad for work, I was looking forward to move back to Italy, I was deeply missing the landscapes, the people and the art. It's really hard to describe in words the warm feeling that gives you walking in the alleys of Rome or drinking a good glass of wine in Tuscany. Those are unique experiences that fill heart with joy and make you daydream.

Even though I've lived in Italy most of my life, this land never ceases to amaze me and make me dream, every small city, every little village is masterpiece.

We are so happy with our country that we love those who come to visit and discover the wonders of this small land.

For Italians there are few basic things in life: love, family and food. We feel really lucky if we have dinner with the people we love, the outside world may even disappear, but good food on the table, good wine and family are enough to be happy.

We are easy people with a big heart and lots of joy. The truth is that we have passion in our blood, we are born surrounded by so much beauty, art, history that there is no Italian in the world that is boring.

So let's start, you will read the sayings, the poems and the most romantic, sweet and beautiful phrases that exist in the Italian language.

Chapter 1

Italian pronounce and phonetic basics

Italian it's "read as it's written".
What does that mean?
Italian spelling is largely phonetic; that is, with only a few exceptions a single letter or cluster of letters represents the same sound, and each sound occurring in the language has only a single written representation.
Because of that, once you learn how to correctly pronounce the vowels and the consonants you'll be able to read *anything*. In fact each letter is pronounced in every word the same way, the A always sound like "fAther". Instead in english fAther, cAt, Able, Apple have different sounds for this vowel.

Another important thing to know about when learning Italian pronunciation is that there are several consonant digraphs in Italian. These are combinations of two letters that make one sound.

So let's cover the basics of phonetic and the pronunciation rules in the Italian language.

Vowels

There are only 5 vowels in the Italian language:

A - E - I - O - U

Italian vowels are *pure*. A sound written with a single letter has a single, unchanged value, whereas in English the sound often changes from one pure sound to another.

Every vowel can either be short or long, depending on the following letters and if they're stressed or not. Vowels that are not stressed are all short, like all the word-ending vowels (except word with the accent mark). For stressed vowels we have two cases:
  • It's long when there are no consonant clusters after: COLA (drip)
  • It's short there are consonant clusters after. COLLA (glue)

Vowel A
Italian **A** is very open and wide. It always sound like: fAther, pApa. It should never sound like *uh* or *aw*.
Amore - Love
"ah-moh-reh"

Vowel E

Italian **E** has two pronunciations, "open" and "closed" sound. Unfortunately there isn't a rule for distinguishing which one to use if you haven't already heard the word pronounced correctly. In fact there are so many little rules that occurs in the way the E is pronounced and it's impossible to cover in just few pages. The best thing is to try with the closed sound as it's the one more frequent.

Open E makes a sound similar to English short E, as in bEt, but a bit more open.

IdEa - Idea

"ee-deh-ah"

Closed E is the most common and is similar to the sound that makes the A in the English word chAos.

Bene - Good

"beh-neh"

Vowel I

Italian **I** is a very easy sound as it already occurs in many English words. It's pronounced like the ee sound in stEEp and never change its pronunciation.

Vino - Wine

"vee-noh"

Vowel O

Italian **O** has the same distinction as the E, it can have an open or closed sound. If the O is at the end of the word is always closed, unless it's stressed (marked with an accent).

Open O makes the sound of the A in Awe, but a lot more open and shrill.

Però - But

"pe-roh"

Closed O is the most common pronunciation and sounds like the O in gO.

Pero - Pear Tree

"pe-ro"

Vowel U

Italian **U** is the rarest vowel, not many words use it. It has a very easy pronunciation, it always sounds like the OO in bOOts.

Umido - Wet

"oo-mee-do"

Diphthongs

Diphthongs are a combination of vowels, like: AI, AE, IO, IU, EO...

Diphthongs are quite frequent in Italian, but if you follow the pronunciation rules above you won't have any problem.

Consonants

Italian and English consonant are pronounced almost the same, but the Italian has different sounds for the C, G, H... and also has double, triple consonants in a row.

So let's see the major differences and how to approach to multiple consonant.

Consonant C and G

Italian **C** has a double sound:

soft C pronounced CH or **hard C** pronounced K.

It all depends on the letter after the C.

C + I/E sounds always CH like in CHeck.

Cibo - Food

"Chi-boh"

C + A/O/U sounds like the English K.

Carino - Cute

"ka-ree-no"

Italian **G** has the same rules to the C. It can sound like J (**soft G**) or G (**hard G**).

G + I/E sounds like J in John:

Gente - People

"jen-teh"

G + A/O/U sounds like a normal G

Gatto - cat

"ga-tto"

There are few common rules:
- C/G + H + vowels make the C/G hard.
- C/G + I + vowels is pronounced without the I
sound. Ciao is pronounced *"cha-o"*.

Consonant H

Italian **H** is always silent in the beginning a word.
However it can change the sound of some consonants
like C or G making it hard as we've just seen.

Consonant Q

Italian **Q** is pronounced as the K in English.

Consonant R

Italian **R** is trilled, no English r-sound is similar.
You need to roll your tongue flipping it against your
upper teeth. It's the most difficult sound to make for
English speakers, so practise over and over again.

Consonant D and T

Italian **D** and **T** are never aspirated, the tongue
should just touch the back of your teeth, not the gums.
The correct pronunciation sound is like the D in
Diamond and the T in Tell.

Consonant Digraphs

Italian has a lot of digraphs, that means a combination of 2 letters that make an unique sound. We already saw CH and GH.
There are some frequent others:
- **GN**: G is silent and N is hard, the word Gnomo (dwarf) is read *"ni-o-mo"*
- **GL**: G is silent, the word Famiglia (family) is read "fah-mee-lee-ah"
- **SC**: + E/I sounds SH like in Pesce (fish) *"pe-she"*
- **SC**: + A/O/U sounds SK like Scarpa (shoe) *"skar-pa"*

Double Consonants

Double consonants are very frequent in Italian. Any Italian consonant can be doubled, except for the H because it's always silent. Double consonants have a stronger and more forced pronunciation together.
Letto - Bed
"leh-t-t-o"

Stress

The majority of Italian words are stressed on the second to last syllable.
The words with an accent mark on the last vowel are always stressed there. On the other hand, the accent is never at the end of the word if there is no mark.

Chapter 2

Common phrases and real world conversation

This is going to be really helpful for anyone who wants to learn a bit of Italian.
Many of the books "Learn Italian Common Phrases" I've seen are completely useless, not because they are wrong grammatically speaking, but simply because nobody in Italy speaks like that.

The "real-world conversations" that are written in those books are old fashioned, and too much formal, and learning that is mostly a waste of time.

Before we immerse ourselves in the poetry of Italian let's see some really useful sentences together.
If you already know them, you can read them out loud to practise the pronunciation or just skip to chapter 4 for the real romantic Italian sayings.

Two short notes about Italian language:
Formal and informal phrases are two ways of saying the same thing, depending to whom you're talking to. The informal way is used when speaking to friends,

family, pets, or more in general to someone you already know. The formal way is to be used with older people, professors and anyone that you don't know (and it's not younger than you).

The other note is about masculine and feminine, in fact each word ends differently if it is referred to a man or a woman. Usually -o is for masculine and -a for feminine. The plural is almost every time ending in -i.

So we are now ready to learn some *true* real-world conversation, greetings, common questions and short everyday dialogues.

PS: you will find even some slang phrases, explained and ready to use. Remember to use them only in a complete informal contest. As Italians we love when people try to speak informal Italian. It always make us laugh, and no, it's not a bad sign, we're not making fun of you, it just fills our heart with joy.

PPS: you can find the audio of the expressions on our website.

Greetings

Ciao
"cha-o"
Hello

Buongiorno
"boo-on-jor-noh"
Good morning

Buona sera
"boo-on-ah—se-rah"
Good evening

Buonanotte
"boo-on-ah—not-te"
Good night

Arrivederci
"a-ri-ve-der-cee"
Bye (formal)

ArrivederLa
"a-ri-ve-der-la"
Goodbye (even more formal)

A dopo
"ah—do-po"
See you later

A presto
"ah—pre-s-to"
See you soon

A fra poco
"ah—frah—poh-ko"
See you really soon

A domani
"ah—doh-mahn-ee"
See you tomorrow

Benvenuti
"ben-ve-noo-tee"
Welcome (formal)

Piacere
"pee-ah-che-reh"
Nice to meet you

SLANG

Ci si becca
"cee—see—be-kka"
See you around

Ci si
"cee—see"
See you around

Both this slang expressions are said between friends after spending few hours together, is less than informal and always said as the very last thing before going different directions.

When you meet someone another common greeting is cheek kissing. Usually it's between people who know each other, like friends or family, and it's more common between women.
If you meet someone for the first time handshakes are the best choice.

Common questions

Come stai?
"ko-meh—stah-ee"
How are you?

Come ti chiami?
"ko-meh—tee—ki-ah-mee"
What's your name?

Quanti anni hai?
"ku-an-tee—an-nee—a-i"
How old are you?

Parli italiano?
"par-lee—ee-tah-lee-ah-no"
Do you speak Italian?

Parli inglese?
"par-lee—ee-n-gle-se"
Do you speak English?

Puoi aiutarmi?
"poo-o-ee—ah-i-oo-tar-mee"
Can you help me?

Mi capisci?
"mee—cah-pee-shee"
Do you understand me?

Desidera qualcosa?
"de-see-de-rah—kual-ko-sah"
Do you want something?
(usually in restaurants or stores, formal)

Come si dice "x" in italiano?
"ko-me—see—di-che—"x"—een—ee-tah-lee-ah-no"
How do you say "house" in Italian?

Dov'è..?
"do-ve-eh"
Where is..?

Da dove vieni?
"da—do-veh—vee-e-nee"
Where are you from?

Dove abiti?
"do-veh—a-bee-tee"
Where do you live?

Common expressions

Grazie mille
"gra-zee-e—meel-le"
Thank you very much

Per favore
"per—fah-voh-reh"
Please

Prego
"pre-goh"
You're welcome

Mi dispiace
"mee—dee-spia-che"
Sorry

Boh
"boh"
I don't know

Scusa
"scoo-sah"
Excuse me (informal)

Mi scusi
"mee—scoo-see"
Excuse me (formal)

Non importa
"non—eem-por-tah"
It doesn't matter

Non ti preoccupare
"non—tee—pre-ok-koo-pah-reh"
Don't worry

Ho fame
"oh—fah-meh"
I'm hungry

Ho sete
"oh—seh-teh"
I'm thirsty

Ho freddo
"oh—freh-doh"
I'm cold

Ho caldo
"oh—kal-doh"
I'm hot

Mi annoio
"mee—an-noh-ee-oh"
I'm bored

Salute
"sah-loo-teh"
Bless you

Congratulazioni
"kon-grah-too-lah-zee-oh-nee"
Congratulations

Buona fortuna
"boo-o-nah—for-too-nah"
Good luck

Va bene
"vah—be-neh"
Okay

Andiamo
"an-dee-ah-mo"
Let's go

Cin cin
"ceen—ceen"
Cheers

Short Dialogues

<u>Greetings between friends informal:</u>

A: Ciao Anna!
"cha-o—an-nah"
B: Ciao Francesca, come stai?
"cha-o—fran-che-scah"
A: Molto bene grazie, e tu?
"mol-toh—be-neh—gra-zee-e"
B: Tutto bene, grazie.
"tut-to—be-neh"

A: Hello Anna!
B: Hi Francesca, how are you?
A: I'm very good, thank you. What about you?
B: Everything's fine, thanks.

<u>Saying goodbye between friends informal:</u>

A: Ciao Chiara, ci vediamo domani
"cha-o—ki-a-rah—cee—ve-dee-a-moh—doh-mah-nee"
B: Ciao Anna, a presto, buonanotte
"cha-o—an-nah—a—pre-sto—boo-o-nah-not-teh"

A: Bye Chiara, see you tomorrow
B: Bye Anna, see you soon, goodnight

<u>Saying goodbye formal:</u>

A: Arrivederci, ci vediamo domani
"a-ri-ve-der-cee—cee—ve-dee-ah-moh—do-mah-nee"
B: ArrivederLa, le auguro una buona serata
*"a-ri-ve-der-lah—le—a-oo-goo-roh—oo-nah—boo-o-nah
—se-rah-tah"*

A: Bye, see you tomorrow
B: Goodbye, I wish you a pleasant evening

<u>Talking about age:</u>

A: Ciao Michela, quanti anni hai?
"cha-o—mee-ke-la—ku-an-tee—an-nee—a-i"
B: Ho otto anni, tu quanti ne hai?
"oh—ot-toh—an-nee—too—ku-an-tee—ne—a-i"
A: Io ne ho venti
"ee-o—ne—oh—ven—tee"
B: Mamma mia, come sei grande!
"mam-mah—mee-ah—ko-meh—se-ee—gran-deh"
A: Si, sono maggiorenne. Tu invece sei ancora piccolina
"si—so-noh—ma-jo-ren-neh—too—een-ve-che—se-ee—an-ko-rah—peek-ko-lee-nah"
B: Si, io sono una bambina
"si—ee-o—so-noh—oo-nah—bam-bee-nah"

A: Hello Michela, how old are you?
B: I'm eight years old, and you?
A: I'm twenty
B: Oh my god, you're so old!
A: Yes, I'm of age. You are still young
B: Yes, I'm a little girl

<u>Asking and giving direction:</u>

A: Mi scusi, mi sa dire dov'è L'Hotel Italia?
"mee—sku-see—mee—sah—dee-reh—do-ve—eh—oh-tel—ee-tah-lee-ah"
B: Si, è in Corso Roma.
"see—eh—een—cor-soh—ro-mah"
A: Mi può spiegare come arrivarci?
"mee—poo-o—spee-e-gah-reh—co-meh—ar-ree-var-cee"
B: Certo, vada avanti per questa strada fino al semaforo, poi giri a sinistra.
"cher-toh—va-dah—a-van-tee—per—ku-e-stah—stra-dah—fee-noh—a-l—se-ma-pho-roh—po-ee—gee-ree—ah—see-nee-strah"
A: Grazie dell'informazione, buona giornata
"gra-zee-e—del—een-phor-ma-zee-oh-neh—boo-o-nah—jor-na-tah"
B: Di niente, arrivederci!
"dee—nee-en-teh—ar-ree-ve-der-cee"

A: I'm sorry, do you know where is Hotel Italia?
B: Yes, it's in Corso Roma
A: Can you give me directions?
B: Sure, go straight until you reach the traffic light, then turn left
A: Thank you for the informations, have a good day
B: You're welcome, goodbye!

Conversation in a restaurant:

A: Un tavolo per due, per favore
"oon—ta-vo-lo—per—doo-eh—per—fa-voh-reh"
B: Prego, si accomodi
"pre-goh—see—ak-koh-moh-dee"
A: Qual è la specialità della casa?
"Kual—eh—lah—spe-cha-lee-tah—de-la—ka-sa"
B: Pasta alla carbonara
"Pa-stah—al-la—car—boh-nah-rah"
A: Perfetto, due paste e un litro di vino
"Per-fet-toh—doo-eh—pah-steh—e—oon—lee-troh—dee—vee-noh"
B: Buon appetito!
"boo-on—ap-peh-tee-toh"

A: A table for two please
B: Here, have a seat
A: What's your most popular dish?
B: Pasta alla Carbonara
A: Well, two pastas and a later of wine
B: Bon appetit!

Chapter 3

Italian idioms and typical expressions

We are getting closer to become real Italians. This idioms are in fact known and used only by Italian native speakers. We're going to go over the most common ones with a full explanation on what they mean. In the next chapter we're finally approaching the romantic Italian expressions.

A buon intenditore poche parole
"a—boo-on—een-ten-dee-to-reh—po-ke—pa-ro-leh"
A word to the wise

Exp: someone smart and intuitive don't need many explanations to understand something. This proverb actually comes from an ancient Latin comedy.

Chi dorme non piglia pesci
"ki—dor-meh—non—pi-g-lee-a—pe-shee"
You snooze, you lose

Exp: means that lazy people, do not get anything.
Just like the fisherman asleep who cannot catch any
fish.
    Literal translation is: who sleeps doesn't get fishes.

A caval donato non si guarda in bocca
*"ah—ka-val—do-nah-toh—non—see—goo-ar-dah—een—
bok-kah"*
Never look in the mouth of a given horse

Exp: This idiom means that complaining about a
gift, or not being happy with it it's rude. In fact if it's a
gift you have to accept it happily and being grateful.
The origin of this proverb comes from long long ago,
when in order to esteem a horse's age you would need
to check its teeth, and that means that checking on the
age of the horse (or in general the quality of the gift)
it's rude towards who gave it to you.

L'erba del vicino è sempre più verde

"l-er-bah—de-l—vee-chee-noh—eh—sem-pre—pee-oo—ver-deh"

The grass is always greener on the other side of the fence

Exp: This expression is about envy. Envious people do not appreciate the good things they have, because they always think that what others have is better.

Il lupo perde il pelo ma non il vizio

"eel—loo-poh—per-deh—eel—pe-loh—ma—non—eel—vee-zee-o"

Old habits die hard

Exp: We are who we are, so no matter how hard we try, at the end of the day we still are ourselves. This means that it is very hard to eradicate habits and vices that are part of our nature. So you can well behave for years, but coming back to a very bad habit. In this case you use this expression. It's also used to warn someone about someone else who is know to have bad vices.

Literal translation is: the wolf lose the fur but non the vice.

Ride bene chi ride ultimo
"ree-de—be-neh—kee—ree-de—ool-tee-moh"
Who laughs last laughs better

Exp: Don't joy about a winning before due time, things can change even the last second. This is a warning, you can use this expression to warn your opponent if it's a challenge, or if you're planning a revenge after you've lost.

Il buon giorno si vede dal mattino
"eel—boo-on-jor-noh—see—ve-deh—dal—mat-tee-noh"
A good day starts from the morning

Exp: This saying means that when a day starts in a good way, it will continue and end in a good way, too. It's actually rarely related to days, this expression has a wider meaning: it's used in every situation, referred to people, actions, football matches, literals anything that looks promising from the very start. It's often used ironically, meaning the opposite: if it's going so bad in the start, imagine how bad will be in the end.

Tra i due litiganti il terzo gode
"tra—ee—doo-e—lee-tee-gan-tee—eel—ter-zoh—go-deh"
Two argue and a third benefits

Exp: This idiom means that when there are two people too busy to argue, usually about something stupid, there is always a third person who takes advantage of the moment and benefits about the thing the other two were arguing about. Can be used in almost every situation, if I'm arguing with you about who takes the last purse in the shop, a friend of ours takes it because we're too busy arguing instead of finding a constructive solution.

Non è tutto oro quel che luccica
"non—eh—toot-toh—oroh—kuel—ke—loo-chi-ka"
All that glitters is not gold

Exp: This means that appearances can be deceiving, it doesn't matter if the surface shines like gold, you need to look at the inside because can just be poor metal. The first impression could be misleading, be careful when judging from the appearances.

In bocca al lupo
"een—bo-kah—al—loo-poh"
To be in the wolf's mouth

Exp: It's used to wish good luck to someone, it's very very common to hear it before school exams, or job interviews. You answer saying "Crepi" that means "hopefully the wolf dies" but it's actually a wrong interpretation. In fact, originally being in the wolf mouth was a good thing, because it's a safe place, but years after has taken on a negative connotations so we just answer "crepi" instead of thank you.

Not many Italians actually know the origin of this expression.

Acqua in bocca
"a-ku-ah—een—bo-kah"
Keep it to yourself

Exp: This expression means that you don't have to spill the beans. I'm telling you something, but you need to take your mouth shut. In Italian we use the water because if you have water in your mouth of course you can't talk.

Literal translation is: keep water in your mouth.

Hai voluto la bicicletta? E adesso pedala!
"a-ee—vo-loo-toh—la—bee-chee-klet-tah—e—a-des-so—pe-da-lah"
You wanted the bike? Now you've got to ride it

Exp: This means that you bought or somehow finally got something that turned out to be more complicated or tiresome that you thought. Ad is usually said ironically after giving them an advice that they didn't followed. It's like saying, I told you so and you did it anyway, now it's your business.

Non vedo l'ora
"non—ve-doh—lo-rah"
Can't wait to

Exp: This is very very very common in real-world conversation. We actually use this expression every time we're excited about something that is going to happen. It means that we can't wait for something to happen in the next future.
Literal translation is: I don't see the hour.

Essere in gamba
"es-se-reh—een—gam-bah"
You are very well-prepared

Exp: This is a weird expressions and not very
common among the younger people. It's an old way of
saying that someone knows what they do, that they're
well-informed and well-prepared on a specific task. It's
always used referred to someone else, you can't say it
about yourself. Translation it's actually weird.
Literal translation is: to be in leg.

Perdere le staffe
"per-de-reh—le—sta-pheh"
To lose the temper

Exp: This means that I'm loosing my calm and
getting very nervous. It's a warning to someone that is
making you mad. It's not really used in conversations,
but you can definitely hear it sometimes.
Literal translation is: to lose the stirrups.

Prendere due piccioni con una fava
"pr-en-de-reh—doo-eh—pee-cho-nee—kon—oo-nah—fa-vah"
Achieve two things with a single action

Exp: This expression is similar to "unisco l'utile e il dilettevole" that means combining business to pleasure, so that in one action I can have both. It's said when you plan things quite well and have found a smart way to do two things with less effort.
Literal translation is: getting two pigeons with a single broad bean.

Essere in alto mare
"e-se-reh—een—al-toh—ma-reh"
Be really behind the schedule

Exp: This means that you still have a long way to go before finishing your project or something you have to do. Usually it's said about school or job tasks.
Literal translation is: being on the high seas.

Rosso di sera bel tempo si spera
"ros-soh—dee—se-rah—bel—tem-poh—see—spe-rah"
Tomorrow there will be good weather

Exp: This is an Italian saying to predict the weather
for the following day. It means that if you have a red
sunset at night then you're likely to have good weather
the next day.
Literal translation is: Red in the evening, good
weather tomorrow.

Non avere peli sulla lingua
"non—a-ve-reh—pe-lee—soo-lah—leen-goo-ah"
Speak your mind

Exp: This means to be straightforward and to speak
your mind directly. This is always referred to someone,
to stand out that he's not afraid of saying what he
believes to be right.
Literal translation is: not having hairs on the
tongue.

Chapter 4

I hope you're starting getting comfortable with Italian expressions, and I'm quite sure that now you have everything you need to fully appreciate the beauty of the Italian sayings.

In this chapter we're going to understand the Italian vision of life, what we value the most, and how we can always be so joyful and relaxed. You'll learn how little things can make huge differences on the way of living.

Giving the right value and the right priorities to the things in our lives keeps the mind clear and the soul lightweight.

So how do you live the Italian way?
We live "La bella vita" that literally means living the good life. Life is one, and rushing makes you lose the beauty of the path, so enjoy you life, find the good in the bad, the ying in the yang, and always take a deep breathe and enjoy the view.

Maybe it's because we're so poetical, or we just love enjoying little things, but we always love the life we're living and not looking for more, more money, more time, more and more and more.

There are some few things that are fundamental for the Italian lifestyle, let's see which ones.

Family. Family it's a blessing for us, spending time all together, enjoying being around, this makes us feel so lucky. It can be the worst day of your life, but going back to the love your family gives you make the day a bit better.

After family and friends comes the food. Food is a huge part of our culture, a lot of the rituals are built around the table. Enjoying lunch or dinner starts from the very beginning, buying the right ingredients, reading the recipes, cooking all together while drinking a glass of wine (note: for the majority of Italians this moments are already the definition of paradise). Then you lay the table and you eat all together, talking about our day, enjoying each other company and drinking a good glass of wine.

Food is the best excuse to see a friend and to tell people you love them. For example saying to someone: "come to my house, I'll make you dinner" it's a very sweet and special invitation, and means they're happy to share time with us. It's kind of easy, if you love someone, offer them a home cooked dinner, it's absolutely the best love declaration.

Third: slow down and relax, when you're having a rough day just stop rushing, take a break, drink a coffe, lay in the sun. You'll feel better. We usually make "Aperitivo" after work, that means that with colleagues or friends you go to a cute cafe and relax. We have a drink with olives, we relax for an hour freeing the mind, and then we go home to have dinner.

Last thing is to be happy. Find something that fills your heart with joy, and just do it. Help people, connect with new ones, chill with friends, be with your loved ones. Find a job you like doing. Money are not the most important things, we'd rather live in a smaller place that giving up on being happy.

"Mangia bene, ridi spesso, ama molto"

Eat well, laugh often, love much

This expression perfectly summarise the Italian way of life. Food, joy and family.

"Quando finisce la partita il re ed il pedone finiscono nella stessa scatola"

When you finish the game, the king and the pawn end up in the same box

In other words: we all meet the same end, so it doesn't matter how big is your house or how many cars you have. Remember to make important and prioritise only the right things in your life.

"Aiutati che Dio ti aiuta"

Help yourself and God will help you

This saying means: start doing it, do not keep waiting
for God's help, He's going to help you when you're
already on the tracks.

"Vendetta mai non sanò piaga"

Revenge never healed a wound

This is a deep reflection on how revenge makes you
feel better at the moment, but doesn't heal the pain of
the wound. To heal you need to forgive.

"Dolce far niente"

The pleasure of idleness

Usually refers to days like Sunday or holiday, when you've worked hard all week and you take your time to relax a full day. You diserve it and you feel empowered by this pleasant feeling of idleness.

"Ho amato le stelle troppo profondamente per avere paura della notte"

I loved the stars too deeply to be afraid of the dark night

This amazing, wonderful saying is so poetic. It means that even if something scares you like the dark, if you love what you do you'll find a way.

"Chi la dura la vince"

He who perseveres wins at last

Who lasts in a challenge, in a difficult situation or in love at the end wins, there's something good that pays for the effort.

"Dai nemici mi guardo io, dagli amici mi guardi Iddio!"

I (will) protect myself from my enemies; may God protect me from my friends!

This is ironic, means that I can forecast that my enemies will do something bad to me, but I trust my friends so I hope they will never be unfair to me, hopefully God will prevent this (meaning that if the friendship is true is also blessed, and no true friend will ever be unfair).

"Chi ben vive, ben muore"

Who lives well, dies well

Means that a life well-lived makes even death not so bad.

"Tempo al tempo"

Literal translation: Time to time
English equivalent: All in good time

Means that the right things will come at the right time, so don't despair if something it's not working yet the way you want it to, when "il tempo sarà maturo" (literal: when the time is ripe, means: at the right time) it will start working and it will even exceed your expectations.

"Tutto è bene quel che finisce bene"

All is well what ends well

Means that everything that has a happy ending is positive, despite the initial difficulties. Also make us forget past hardships when these have not brought irreparable damage.

"Vedi Napoli e poi muori"

See Naples, and then die

This is actually a very beautiful expressions, means that Naples is so beautiful that going away is compared to death. Nowhere else you will find amazing places, people and food like in Naples, is so unique that leaving make you melancholic.

"Non puoi insegnare niente a un uomo. Puoi solo aiutarlo a scoprire ciò che ha dentro di sé"

You cannot teach a man anything, you can only help find it within himself

This means that everyone has its own way to learn, and to teach something to someone it's necessary to find the right way to speak to them. To ignite something inside of them.

"Se non hai mai pianto, i tuoi occhi non possono essere belli"

If you haven't cried, your eyes can't be beautiful

This means that after a great pain you find an awareness that makes you more beautiful. There's no true beauty without a big sorrow.

"Una cena senza vino e come un giorno senza sole"

A meal without wine is a day without sunshine

This means that after a great pain you find an awareness that makes you more beautiful. There's no true beauty without a big sorrow.

"Quando il diavolo ti accarezza, vuole l'anima"

When the devil caresses you, he wants your soul

This means that the opportunists are very kind only for a second purpose, that is, they want to get something from us. So be careful, devil wants always something back.

"Vecchi peccati hanno le ombre lunghe"

Old sins have long shadows

This is a warning, it means that no matter how hard you try to hide your sins, year after year they "grow their shadows", you need to lie on lies until they consume you.

"Meglio soli che male accompagnati"

Better alone than in bad company

This saying means that even if you're sad because of being alone, it's always better than being surrounded by fake friends or people that spend time with you only to exploit you.

"Dopo la pioggia, arriva il sole"

After the rain comes sunshine

Don't worry too much about the present, better times
will come. So if you are in a bad situation right now,
hold on and keep going, it will come the sun.

"Vino rosso fa buon sangue"

Red wine makes good blood

This saying comes to an old (and wrong) belief that
red wine helps the blood be more red and "good". The
truth is that we love wine so much that we make up
this kind of things to feel legitimated. In fact drinking
too much red wine is actually harmful for our blood.
But, and it's a big but, only a glass of wine a day
instead is good for our body (and our souls).

"A tavola non si invecchia"

At the table, you don't get old

This is actually this is so Italian. Eating at the table, maybe with the family, it's such a pleasure that feels like time is not going by. Time freezes and we're not getting older.

"Fuggi il piacer presente, che accenna dolor futuro"

Escape the present pleasure that hints future pain

Skip the enjoyment that you will regret in future. This warns you to think twice about what you're going to do, if something seems so good right now but you have a feeling that you're going to regret it in the future don't do it.

"Ogni cosa ha cagione"

Everything has a reason

This saying explains itself, it means that everything has a hidden reason, so even if you don't see it right now, have faith and you'll find out why it's happening.

"Buon seme dà buoni frutti"

Good seed makes good fruit

This is similar to another proverb: "Buon sangue non mente" - Good blood doesn't lie. They have the same meaning that is: if the base is solid, so a good seed that comes from great plants, or good blood from a good family, chances are that also the new seed/blood will continue the previous prestige.

"Chi due lepri caccia, l'una non piglia e l'altra lascia"

Literal: who hunts two hares, doesn't catch one and makes the other run away
English equivalent: Grasp all, lose all

This is similar to another proverb: "Chi troppo vuole nulla stringe" - Who wants too much gets nothing. They both mean that you need to choose and focus on one thing and aim to that, if you're too assumptive you'll end up with nothing.

"Uomo avvisato, mezzo salvato"

Forewarned is forearmed

It has the exact same meaning than in English. I warned you, now you have to do your part in saving yourself.

"Tra il dire e il fare c'è di mezzo il mare"

Literal translation: There's a sea between saying and doing
English equivalent: Easier said than done

This means that orally we can make amazing projects and speculations, and just talking feels so easy, but doing it for real it's the hard part. You'll find along the way many obstacles you haven't even pictured before starting doing it.

"Quel ch'è fatto, è fatto"

What is done is done

Means that once something it's done, you can go back. So think about the right decisions to take so you won't regret them after.

"Chi fa da sé, fa per tre"

Literal translation: who does it by itself does it for three people
English equivalent: Do it yourself if you want it done right

According to this proverb, if a person starts a business on his own, he may be able to do it surprisingly well, better than if there were three people involved but with less motivation or skills.

"O la va, o la spacca"

All or Nothing

This is used when you are in an important or difficult situation and you have to make a choice, even if you are not sure of the success. Therefore you decide to try all or nothing by taking on your responsibility for the choice.

"Chi niente sa, di niente dubita"

Who knows nothing, doubts nothing

This saying means that the less you know, the less curious you are, the less doubt you have. It's because you're not interested in finding out more about the world and so you don't even have questions or doubts.

"Tutte le verità sono facili da capire una volta che sono state rivelate. Il difficile è scoprirle"

All truths are easy to understand once they are discovered. What is difficult is to discover them

This phrase means that once you've find out the truth it all makes sense, but the difficult part is putting the pieces together.

"Meglio tardi che mai"

Better late than never

Usually it's said as ironic comment for the delay with which something that we have been waiting for finally happens, but more commonly it's used when someone is really late and finally shows up.

"Altro il vino non è se non la luce del sole mescolata con l'umido della vite"

Wine is nothing but sunlight mixed with the grapevine

This is a poetic saying about wine, it means that wine is such a magic thing that is done with sunlights.

"Vivi e lascia vivere"

Live and let live

This is an invitation not to annoy others with intrusive and critical behaviour. You can give wise advices, of course, but your opinion is not the only one right, so don't judge what others do.

"Non ho mai incontrato un uomo così ignorante dal quale non abbia potuto imparare qualcosa"

I have never met a man ignorant to such an extent that I could not learn something from him

This saying is very deep, means that everybody can teach you something, so be humble and listen to others. Even a child can teach you something you didn't know.

"La superstizione porta sfortuna"

Superstition brings misfortune

This is a warning, means that if you believe something negative and dark, somehow something bad will happen to you. On the other side if you are optimistic you will attract good things.

"Colui che vede un bisogno e aspetta che gli venga chiesto aiuto è scortese quanto colui che lo rifiuta"

A person who sees a need and waits to be asked for help is as unkind as a person who refuses to give it

This means that knowing that if someone needs help and you act like nothing it's happening it's even worse than being asked for help and refuse.

"La lettura è un'immortalità all'indietro"

Reading is immortality backwards

Each reading is an experience and an adventure: we stop being ourselves and become something else. So if you read you'll live hundreds of lives, if you don't you'll only live one: yours.

"Non importa se si procede lentamente, l'importante è non fermarsi"

 It does't matter how slowly you go as long as you do not stop

This explains itself. It means that even if you are doing something slowly, maybe not reaching the goals you thought you'd be reaching, keep going and have faith.

***"Il miglior momento per piantare un albero era 20 anni fa. Il secondo miglior momento è ora"**

The best time to plant a tree was 20 years ago. The second best time is now

This saying intends to encourage people to start doing what they want right now. Anyone can be afraid that "it's too late to start this know" because maybe there is more competition in business or you're too young, but you don't have to wait any longer. Do it know, it's the best time.

*"Non si può mai attraversare l'oceano
se non si ha il coraggio di perdere di
vista la riva"*

You can never cross the ocean until you have
the courage to lose sight of the shore

This means that if you stay in your comfort zone you'll
never be able to achieve impossible things, so even if
it's scary do it, lose the sight of the safe zone, and
you'll do amazing things.

"Non ci sono scorciatoie verso qualsiasi posto in cui valga la pena di andare"

There are no shortcuts to any place worth going

You can take shortcuts to do simple things, you can even cheat in your exams or at work, but you will never find shortcuts if you want to build something extraordinary. Because it takes real effort, time, sweat, and there is no way to bypass that.

Chapter 5

We've seen some interesting sayings about Italian lifestyle, but to fully understand Italian way of thinking we need to read about family, friends and love.

For us Italians, family is such a blessing that even words are not enough to describe it. So we rely on poets and writers who describe these things with exciting words.

"La famiglia non è una cosa importante. È tutto"

Family is not an important thing. It's everything

This is the essence of what we think about family. Having a family means everything, they will always be there for you.

"La famiglia è la patria del cuore"

Family is the homeland of the heart.

This means that everything is about family, all our hearts are filled with family love. Family means being always supported and loved.

"Una buona mamma vale cento maestre"

A good mother is worth a hundred teachers.

Teachers are of course fundamental for the child's growth, this saying means that a good mom that loves her baby will teach him good lessons about life, love and everything you won't learn in school.

"L'affetto verso i genitori è fondamento di ogni virtù"

Loving one's parents is fundamental to all the greatest virtues

This saying means that everything starts with the family, every virtue you'll learn start by loving your parents and be kind.

"Chi si volta, e chi si gira, sempre a casa va finire"

No matter where you go or turn, you'll always end up at home.

No matter what you do, no matter if you've lost all the contacts with your family or you've argued few years ago, there will be a moment in your life where you'll go back to them.

"A ogni uccello il suo nido è bello"

Literal translation: every bird finds his own nest
beautiful
English equivalent: home sweet home

This means that even if your house isn't big, or you
have a small weird family, there's nothing like home.

"I fratelli uniti tra loro formano un fascio che può resistere agli sforzi più robusti"

The brothers joined together form a beam that
can resist the most robust efforts

This could be translated like: united we stand, divided
we fall. The love shared between brothers is so strong
that nothing can break it. Union is strength.

"La mia famiglia è la mia forza e la mia debolezza"

My family is my strength and my weakness

Family is everything. I can rely on them and I know that whatever happens in my life they will be there, for this they are my strength. They are also my weakness because if anything happens to them or someone treats them badly I would do anything to rescue them, in fact anything that concerns them hurts differently.

"Quando arrivano i problemi, è la famiglia che ti sostiene"

When problems come, it is the family that supports you

Family will be there for you for lifetime.

"Amor di madre, amore senza limiti"

Mother's love, love without limits

A mother's love has no limits, a mother will do anything for her kids and will love them unconditionally even if they're not behaving well. It's a pure love that will withstand the hardships of life.

"Un bimbo che non gioca, felicità ne ha poca"

A child that doesn't play, has little happiness

This means that a healthy kid is supposed to play all day long and only think about that. If a child needs to worry for adult problems means that there's a problem. No kid should be thinking about responsibilities, food, bad parenting and more.

"Le piante vogliono essere annaffiate, ma non affogate"

Literal translation: plants want to be taken care of, not suffocated
English equivalent: over-protection does more harm than good

This saying means that plants (children) need to learn basic things from parents or teachers, but they also need to think with their own mind. So don't impose your ideas to your child, make suggestions but never impositions.

"La famiglia è uno dei capolavori della natura"

The family is one of nature's masterpieces

There is no explanation needed. Family is a blessing.

"Solo i veri amici ti diranno quando il tuo viso è sporco"

Only true friends will tell you when your face is dirty

This means that if you're doing something wrong, or you behave badly they will say it to your face. All the other people will just pretend they like you or your behaviour and then they secretly criticise you.

"L'amicizia raddoppia le gioie e divide le angosce"

Friendship doubles the joys and divides the anxieties

Having friends is so important, you can share good and bad moments. They will rejoice with you when something good happens, and they will show you their support in bad times.

"Gli amici ascoltano quello che dici. I migliori amici ascoltano quello che non dici"

Friends listen to what you say. Best friends listen to what you don't say

This means that everybody can listen to what you say, if you ask for help or other. But true best friends will know that you need help even before you seek for it.

"Un'amicizia finita non è mai stata sincera"

A friendship that ends has never been sincere

This is extreme but means that true and deep friendships will overcome any obstacle and last forever. On the other hand normal friendship will end at the first difficulties.

"Una delle più gran consolazioni di questa vita è l'amicizia; e una delle consolazioni dell'amicizia è quella di avere qualcuno a cui confidare un segreto"

One of the greatest consolations of this life is friendship; and one of the consolations of friendship is having someone to share a secret with

This means that friendship gladdens the soul. If you have a secret that weighs on your shoulders you can share it with your friends. The secret will weight less and you'll feel relieved.

"Nessuna cosa è bella da possedere se non si hanno amici con cui condividerla"

No thing is nice to own if you don't have friends to share it with

Like a famous movie: happiness is real only when shared. There is no point in having a great car, or big house, or new game consoles if you don't have someone to share it with.

"Nessun impegno è più importante di un amico che bussa alla porta"

No commitment is more important than a friend who knocks on the door

This means that when a friend asks for help you need to be there for him.

"Un amico è una persona che conosce i tuoi punti sensibili ma non li colpirà mai"

A friend is someone who knows your sensitive points but will never hit them

This is friendship, you know the worst things, the secrets and a lot of bad stuff but you'll never ever tell anyone. Friendship is about loyalty, and a true friend will never hurt you on purpose.

"Le amicizie devono essere immortali, e mortali le inimicizie"

Friendships must be immortal, mortal shall be the enmities

This means that if one is a true friend puts errors aside for the sake of friendship.

"Riprendi l'amico in segreto e lodalo in pubblico"

Scold your friend in secret and praise him in public

This is similar to "Solo i veri amici ti diranno quando il tuo viso è sporco", and means that friends are honest and loyal, so they will always put a good word for you in front of other people, but in private they will point you out your mistakes.

Quando l'amico chiede, non v'è domani.

When a friend asks, there is no tomorrow.

This expression is similar to the one we've seen before: "Nessun impegno è più importante di un amico che bussa alla porta" and means that helping a friend when he needs it is the most important thing.

"Finché abbiamo dei ricordi, il passato dura. Finché abbiamo delle speranze, il futuro ci attende. Finché abbiamo degli amici, il presente vale la pena di essere vissuto"

As long as we have memories, the past lasts. As long as we have hopes, the future awaits us. As long as we have friends, the present is worth living.

This is the sweetest quote about friendship. Friends make the present worth it, so if you have a very bad day just keep in mind the people that love you.

"Se qualcuno ti resta accanto nei momenti peggiori, allora merita di essere con te nei momenti migliori"

If someone stays with you in the worst moments, then they deserve to be with you in the best ones

This amazing saying summarise what friendship is, a noble feeling made of loyalty, joy and support.

Chapter 6

Italian sayings about love

Love, love and love. Love is what that wakes us up in the morning and makes us fall asleep in the evening with a smile. Love is the reason for everything. There is no life without love, there would be no sunrise, there would be no music. For us Italians love it's simply the only thing that matters the most. Love ignites us and makes us better people.

Love, passion, desire.

It's the only thing worth living for.
So just allow yourself to love, open your heart to your family, to your friends, to strangers. There are so many way of loving. The important thing is to never give up on love, no matter how hurt you are.

So here we are, let's see what Italian people think about love, and how has been described by Italian authors.

"Ti amo"

I love you

This is the the easiest and deepest way to tell someone
you love them. You can add:
"Ti amo moltissimo" = I love you so much
"Ti amo con tutto il mio cuore" = I love you with my
whole heart
"Ti amo amore mio" = I love you my love

"L'amore è cieco"

Love is blind

This means that love does not follow logical or
rational criteria, therefore it happens that we love
people who we shouldn't like and we don't know why it
happens to us. You can fall in love with a person that is
absolutely not your type, because love happens and
you can't do anything about it.

"L'amor che muove il sole e l'altre stelle"

Love which moves the sun and other stars of heaven

It's the last verse of Heaven and Divine Comedy by Dante Alighieri. Dante embodies the meaning of the whole work, of God, of the universe, in the fact that love is the mechanism of the world and of life.

"Nè Creator né creatura fu mai senza amore"

Neither Creator nor creature was ever without love

This is also from Divine Comedy. Love is the element that qualifies each human being, starting with God Himself who is Pure Love.

"L'amore vince sempre"

Literal translation: Love always wins
English equivalent: Love conquers all

This means that between good and evil or between love and hate, Love will always wins. Love is more powerful than hate, being able to forgive, being able to accept are all different form of love.

"Il mio amore per te è come l'universo: non avrà mai fine"

My love for you is like the universe: it will never end

This is so poetic and sweet. As big as the universe, as infinite as the universe, our love is. This is a perfect way to tell someone you will love him/her forever.

"La buona moglie fa il buon marito"

A good wife makes a good husband

This is an old saying and means that being a good partner (either wife or husband) is essential for a successful marriage. Don't judge your loved one, in fact try to be a good partner first. This will start fixing a lot of things.

"Amor, ch'a nullo amato amar perdona"

Love, that exempts no one beloved from loving

This is another verse of the Divine Comedy. Passionate love is described, which overwhelms the senses and does not allow a person who is truly loved not to reciprocate the feeling; love is such intense, that even after death it resists.

"Beati coloro che si baceranno sempre al di là delle labbra, varcando il confine del piacere, per cibarsi dei sogni"

Blessed are those who will always kiss beyond the lips, crossing the border of pleasure, to feed on dreams

This amazing verse of the poetry of Alda Merini means that true love goes beyond the physical dimension, goes beyond the lips to reach the soul.

"Amare ed essere saggi è impossibile"

To love and to be wise is impossible

This is because when we're in love we tend not to be rational, looking at things through the filter of love.

"Il vero amore è come una finestra illuminata in una notte buia. Il vero amore è una quiete accesa"

True love is like a window lit on a dark night. True love is a lit quiet

It describes the miracle that happens when a love lasts over time, one of the most precious feelings in life. True love is not always overwhelming, but during the years is soft and everlasting.

"Non assomigli più a nessuna da quando ti amo"

You haven't looked like anyone since I love you

Think about someone you love. They are unique, they are irreplaceable. They are full of small details that no one else in the world has.

*"Il vero amore deve sempre far male.
Deve essere doloroso amare qualcuno,
doloroso lasciare qualcuno…solo
allora si ama sinceramente"*

True love must always hurt. It must be painful
to love someone, painful to leave someone ...
only then we love each other sincerely

This means that when you find your other half, you'll
suffer a lot. You'll have to accept things you don't like
and feelings will be hurt. But if it's true love is always
worth it.

"Ci si abbraccia per ritrovarsi interi"

We embrace each other to find ourselves whole

This means that we need to embrace our loved ones to
feel good, to feel whole again.

"L'amore tutto dimentica, tutto perdona, dà tutto senza riserve"

Love forgets everything, forgives everything, gives everything without reservations

Love is everything, true love can't be partial. If you truly love someone you will always forgive them in the name of love.

"Il sole è la vita della terra, l'amore è la vita dell'uomo e tu, cara, sei la mia vita perché io t'amo"

The sun is the life of the earth, the love is the life of the man and you, my dear, you are my life because I love you

So romantic. No explanation needed. Just read it few times to fully appreciate the beauty of this verse.

"Sarei perduto s'io vivessi un solo momento senza di te"

I would be lost if I lived a single moment without you

This a perfect dedication to your loved one. It holds and describes the feeling of love.

"Il vero amore può nascondersi, confondersi, ma non può perdersi mai"

True love can be hidden, mistaken, but it can never be lost

There are times when two lovers need to separate, but if it's true love, they will find a way.

"Dio mio, spiegami amore come si fa ad amare la carne senza baciarne l'anima"

My God, my love explain to me how you can love the flesh without kissing its soul

To love the flesh only is not love. It is attraction, it is passion, it is carnality. It is not love. Love is another thing, it's understanding the totality of the other person.

"Nessuno è felice come chi sa di essere amato"

Nobody is happy as someone who knows he is loved

Being love makes you brave and happy. Knowing that at the end of the day, no matter what, someone loves you is the best feeling in the world.

"Certi tramonti non tramontano mai"

Some sunsets never sets

This saying has a romantic meaning. It means that even if a love story is over, there is a chance that will resume after some time.

"Certi amori fanno giri immensi e poi ritornano"

Certain loves make huge turns and then return

This has the same meaning as the one above. If it's true love it'll come back, even after a huge turn.

"Per sempre tua"

Forever yours

How beautiful can be just 3 words. Amazing.

"Chi ha l'amor nel petto, ha lo sprone a'fianchi"

He who has love in his chest, has spurs in his sides

This means that if you are in love with someone you won't fear anything. Love is the fuel, like spurs for horses.

Italian Love Poetries

Quando saremo due saremo veglia e sonno,
affonderemo nella stessa polpa
come il dente di latte e il suo secondo,
saremo due come sono le acque, le dolci e le
salate,
come i cieli, del giorno e della notte,
due come sono i piedi, gli occhi, i reni,
come i tempi del battito
i colpi del respiro.
Quando saremo due non avremo metà
Saremo un due che non si può dividere con
niente.
Quando saremo due, nessuno sarà uno,
uno sarà l'uguale di nessuno
e l'unità consisterà nel due.
Quando saremo due
cambierà nome pure l'universo
diventerà diverso.

*When we'll be two, we'll be like sleep and
watch,
we'll sink in the same flesh, like the milk
tooth and its successor,
we'll be two like the waters, the fresh and
the salt one,
like the skies, nocturnal and diurnal,
two like the feet, the eyes, the kidneys,
like the heart beat times and the breath
blows.
When we'll be two, we'll have no halves,
we'll be a two that nothing can divide.
When we'll be two, nobody will be one,
one will be the equal of no one,
the unity will consist of the two.
When we'll be two
we'll change the name even the UNIverse,
it will become TWOverse.*

Due, Erri De Luca

Senza di te un albero
non sarebbe più un albero.
Nulla senza di te
sarebbe quello che è.

Without you a tree
it would no longer be a tree.
Nothing without you
would be what it is.

A Rina, Giorgio Caproni

Accarezzami, amore,
ma come il sole
che tocca la dolce fronte della luna.
Non venirmi a molestare anche tu
con quelle sciocche ricerche
sulle tracce del divino.
Dio arriverà all'alba
se io sarò tra le tue braccia.

Caress me, love,
but like the sun
that touches the sweet forehead of the moon.
Don't come and harass me too
with those silly searches
on the traces of the divine.
God will arrive at dawn
if I am in your arms.

Alda Merini

Rimani! Riposati accanto a me.
Non te ne andare.
Io ti veglierò. Io ti proteggerò.
Ti pentirai di tutto fuorchè d'essere venuto a
me, liberamente, fieramente.
Ti amo. Non ho nessun pensiero che non sia
tuo;
non ho nel sangue nessun desiderio che non
sia per te.
Lo sai. Non vedo nella mia vita altro
compagno, non vedo altra gioia
Rimani.
Riposati. Non temere di nulla.
Dormi stanotte sul mio cuore.

Stay!
Rest beside me.
Do not go.
I will watch you. I will protect you.
Do you regret anything but for coming to
me, freely, proudly.
I love you. I do not have any thought that is
not yours;
I have no desire in the blood that is not for
you.
You know. I do not see in my life another
companion, I see no other joy
Stay up.
Rested. Do not be afraid of anything.
Sleep tonight on my heart.

Rimani, D'Annunzio

We are at the end of our journey through the Italian sayings. I hope that you've learned a lot with me, and are willing to learn each day more about Italy.

Reading these verse, quotes, idioms and sayings is truly inspiring. The way authors describe feeling as love and life is so impressive.

If you are passionate and want to know more about Italy and Italian culture, come to **neeoart.com/italy** website. You can also find the audio of everything written here.

I would like to leave you with one of my favorite poem about love. It is a bit complex to translate all the nuances into another language but I am sure you'll be able to appreciate its beauty anyway.

*Ho sceso, dandoti il braccio, almeno un
milione di scale
e ora che non ci sei è il vuoto ad ogni
gradino.
Anche così è stato breve il nostro lungo
viaggio.
Il mio dura tuttora, né più mi occorrono
le coincidenze, le prenotazioni,
le trappole, gli scorni di chi crede
che la realtà sia quella che si vede.*

*Ho sceso milioni di scale dandoti il braccio
non già perché con quattr'occhi forse si
vede di più.
Con te le ho scese perché sapevo che di noi
due
le sole vere pupille, sebbene tanto offuscate,
erano le tue.*

*I went down a million stairs, at least, arm in
arm with you.
And now that you are not here, I feel
emptiness at each step.
Our long journey was brief, though.
Mine still lasts, but I don't need
any more connections, reservations,
 traps, humiliation of those who think reality
is what we are used to see.*

*I went down a millions of stairs, at least,
arm in arm with you,
and not because with four eyes we see better
that with two.
With you I went downstairs because I knew,
among the two of us,
the only real eyes, although very blurred,
belonged to you.*

Eugenio Montale

È stato emozionante,
grazie.